**M.N. Sahulamid, Regina Bagam**

.

# Accuracy in selecting reconfigurable web services

## Dynamic web services

GRIN Verlag

**Bibliografische Information der Deutschen Nationalbibliothek:**

Die Deutsche Bibliothek verzeichnet diese Publikation in der Deutschen National-
bibliografie; detaillierte bibliografische Daten sind im Internet über http://dnb.d-
nb.de/ abrufbar.

**Imprint:**

Copyright © 2013 GRIN Verlag GmbH
Druck und Bindung: Books on Demand GmbH, Norderstedt Germany
ISBN: 978-3-656-51590-6

**This book at GRIN:**

http://www.grin.com/en/e-book/262732/accuracy-in-selecting-reconfigurable-web-
services

**GRIN - Your knowledge has value**

Der GRIN Verlag publiziert seit 1998 wissenschaftliche Arbeiten von Studenten, Hochschullehrern und anderen Akademikern als eBook und gedrucktes Buch. Die Verlagswebsite www.grin.com ist die ideale Plattform zur Veröffentlichung von Hausarbeiten, Abschlussarbeiten, wissenschaftlichen Aufsätzen, Dissertationen und Fachbüchern.

**Visit us on the internet:**

http://www.grin.com/

http://www.facebook.com/grincom

http://www.twitter.com/grin_com

# Accuracy in selecting reconfigurable web services

- M N Sahulamid ME , M Regina Bagam MCA ME

**ABSTRACT:**

Service-Oriented Architecture (SOA) provides a flexible framework for service composition. Using standard-based protocols (such as SOAP and WSDL).There are several constraints meant for selecting the right and appropriate service to be designed as reconfigurable dynamic web services. Those constraints leverage to the following factors availability, response time, failure handling and supports dynamic configuration. Our paper presents the way of predicting the service methods which are really necessary for providing as a dynamic web service. Since all the service methods cannot be used as dynamically as it depends upon the number of users really using the service by the service providers.

**INTRODUCTION FOR SELECTING DYNAMIC WEB SERVICES:**

Web Services are software applications or services that are uniquely identified by a URI (Uniform Resource Identifiers) and expose public interfaces for clients, using XML (extended markup language). Those web services can be discovered and used by other client applications using XML based messages and protocols such as HTTP.

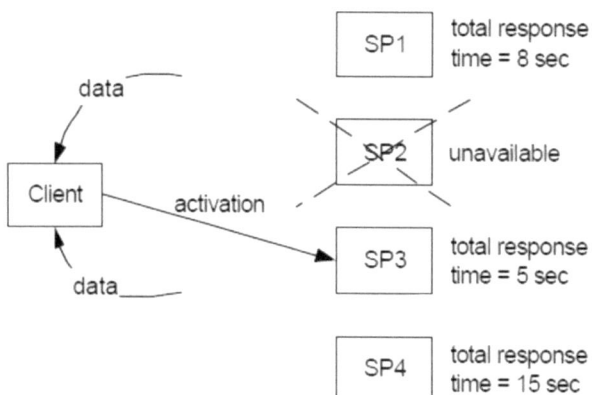

Figure 1 – web service activation according to response time and availability

The emergence and continued development of web services standards such as SOAP (simple object access protocol) and WSDL (web services description language) [3] enable us to request and describe web services in a standard way.

This will increase the ease of use of web services, enable interoperability between heterogeneous platforms and help businesses solve integration problems of their applications. Consequently, it is anticipated that web servers that host the services will be subject to increasing usage and have a higher load. Furthermore, the current simple modulus operand involving client/server activation of a single web service will be enhanced to support more complex scenarios, in which applications and service providers themselves rely on other external web services as part of their business logic. The reliance on third party web services reduces the control of the Organization over its application and (sometimes) mission-critical code. The control and information of certain parts of the system is pushed outside organizational boundaries. Scenarios involving reliance on external web services raise several new issues and challenges. An example of common scenario would be of clients consuming external web services, which in turn outsource their computational resources to other service providers. Furthermore, runtime information such as service load and availability or business related constraints might affect the selection process of an external web service, and not be pre decided, as it is today. In the existing frameworks for web services there is no incentive to bind dynamically to a specific web service. However, once runtime information concerning those web services is available to the application, a dynamic binding becomes advantageous over a static, pre-decided one. We suggest a model that provides the web service client runtime information that is pertinent to its execution and business logic. The client application can then dynamically bind to the temporarily best service, from a selection of acceptable web services it works with, and according to the client's set of constraints. A client may want to apply some business rules when dynamically choosing a web service, or may be more concerned with response time or availability. When response time is critical (e.g. stock quotes service etc.) it is important for an application to activate the fastest web service available at that given time, or have some mechanism that ensures availability and reliability. When several clients participate in such a scenario, an indirect load balancing mechanism is created, which helps to direct clients to available and relatively fast web services.

Figures 1 illustrate a client activation decisions based on information gathered at runtime from the service providers according to the client constraints.

In figure 1, the client is concerned with availability and response times of a web service; after retrieving related information from the service providers, it activates the fastest available web service. This behavior contributes to the robustness of the client application. Figure 1 shows client activation, based on response time and quality of service. According to the client's business constraints, it may prefer to switch to another service provider when it observes a change in the combination of quality and response time offered by the service providers.

**RELATED WORK:**
**Architecture**

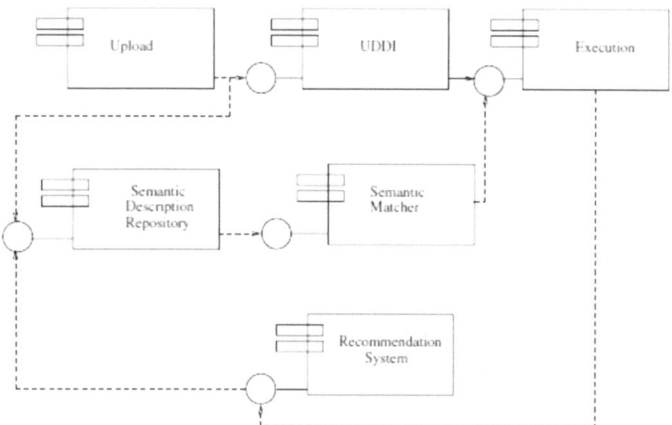

**Figure 2. Architecture of the Dynamic Web Service Selection Framework**

Figure 2 shows different components involved in a Dynamic web service selection Framework. The upload component uploads semantic description and WSDL parameters of a web service. The information from WSDL document is extracted and stored in UDDI repository. The semantic matcher matches semantic descriptions of services with user requirements and proposes a list of services matching with his requirements. The user can execute any of matching services using execution environment. The recommendation component asks the user to rate the executed service, so it will be used for recommendation purpose.

**Semantic Matcher**

Service providers publish DAML-S [5] descriptions of services to a Semantic Description Repository. A service user gives his requirements using DAML-S description. The semantic matcher finds the match between user requirement and all published service descriptions using a Semantic Matching Algorithm. It along with Recommendation System gives matching services in an order.

Figure 3 shows the detailed architecture of a Semantic Matcher [6][7][4]. The Ontology Inference Engine creates a knowledge base from the specified ontology in a DAML-S description and a request description. Web Service Description parser parses theWeb Service Descriptions to find out different parameters to be matched. The criteria table specifies service attributes to be compared and the

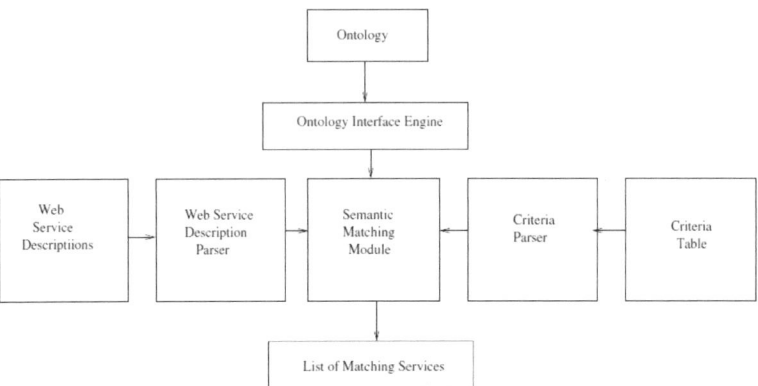

least preferred similarity measures for those attributes. The similarity measure can be exact, plug-in, subsumption, container, disjoint, part of. If the two conceptual annotations are syntactically identical, the mapping is called an Exact map. If the second conceptual annotation specializes the first, the mapping is called Plug-in. If the first conceptual annotation specializes the second, the mapping is called Subsumption map.

If the first conceptual annotation contains the second, the mapping is called a Container map and if first conceptual annotation is part of the second, the mapping is called Part of map. Otherwise the mapping is called disjoint map.

**Recommendation System**

The Dynamic Web Service Selection Framework has a recommendation system, which recommends the best service satisfying the user's requirements. When a user uses a web service, it asks user to rate a web service; so that users can help each other to find a better web service. This is especially important when there are more than one web services which have same functionality but their quality of service is different. We provide the user, a metric to help him decide the rating of a web service. It will be a comparison matrix of runtime behavior of a web service and the users expected QoS parameters like max execution time, average execution time, max response time, average response time etc. Web service with better quality of service will get more rating than other service which offers same functionality but poor service quality. The recommendation system uses the item based collaborative filtering approach [8]. As users rate web services, it is possible to predict how a given user will rate a particular web service. Once it knows prediction of ratings to each web service satisfying user requirements, it can recommend web services in order of their ratings. This approach looks at the set of web services the target user has rated and computes how similar they are to the web service for which user rating is to be predicted. Once the similar web services are found, the prediction is computed by taking a weighted average of the target user's ratings on these similar web services. The item based collaborative filtering approach has two aspects namely similarity computation and prediction generation.

## 1. Similarity Computation

The similarity [8][9] between two web services is computed by subtracting the average rating of the two web services. Considering only users who have rated both web service A and web service B, say that there are 10 such users, we sum the ratings that A and B got, say 65 and 85. Clearly B is ranked higher than A by 2 on average. The similarity between web services is computed whenever users rate a web service. The result of similarity computation is stored in a similarity matrix.

## 2. Prediction Generation

The prediction function [8][9] predicts how a particular user will rate a web service. It computes prediction on a web service i for a user u by computing the sum of ratings given by the user on the web services similar to i. Each rating is weighted by the corresponding similarity $Si,j$ between web services i and j. $Pu,i = $ _all similar items, j($si,j * Ru,j$) _all similar items, j($|si,j|$) Basically it tries to capture how the active user rates the similar web services. The weighted sum is scaled by the sum of the similarity terms to make sure the prediction is within the predefined range. If the user has used a similar service, it predicts his likely satisfaction index for this service/service chain. If no similar service has been used before, it considers the average rating of all the users for similar services.

## DYNAMIC SERVICE SELECTION BASED ON RANKING

The aim of this phase is selecting the best services for the near-optimal compositions such that 1)consider the best quality regard to the user's demand and 2) the composition of these services has high functionality.

## Considering the Most Eligible Services

In order to select services for the near-optimal compositions we use the utility function that we have computed from the result of the classification part. So we do not consider all the possible combinations of services. In this regard, we just mention the candidate services that have a utility value over a defined threshold. This threshold allows us to focus on the most qualified services to our regard. For defining threshold we consider two aspects: the number of required compositions and the execution time of the algorithm. Indeed, if we decrease the value of this threshold, the number of considered candidate services decreases. Consequently, the number of compositions and the execution time of the algorithm decreases respectively. Tuning the trade-off between these two aspects will make our algorithm adaptable; hence it could be applied to multiple dynamic service environments according to their constraints.

**Functional Aspect of the Composition**

Unlike most of approaches which just focus on the quality of composition by means of nonfunctional parameters, the quality of semantic links can be considered as a distinguishing functional criterion for semantic web service compositions. Here we focus on the functional level of composing the candidate web services. The functional criteria of semantic link, was introduced for the first time in which defined as a semantic connection between an output of a service and an input parameter of another service. Since the qualities of these connections are valued by a semantic matching between their parameters, semantic link composition could be estimated and ranked as well. Through the results of these estimations some compositions are inappropriate. Indeed a composite service which does not provide acceptable quality of semantic links might be useless as a service that does not provide the desired functionality. Indeed the semantic connection between Web services is considered as essential to form new value-added Web services. Here we address the problem of optimizing in service selection with respect to this functional criterion. In other words, we focus on the aspects of selecting a set of appropriate service candidates for each task. We define an objective function In order to consider this aspect, preferences and constraints which are defined by end-user.

**SERVICE SELECTION ALGORITHMS FOR GENERAL FLOW STRUCTURE**

Many real-world service processes have services that are not in strictly sequential order. They may have parallel operations to perform several services at the same time, conditional branch operations, and loops for using a service more than once in a flow. The function graph for composite service with general composition patterns may contain complex structures among function nodes. In order to simplify the problem and construct a service candidate graph with a DAG structure, we first remove the loop operations by unfolding the cycles as in [Zeng et al. 2004]. A cycle is unfolded by cloning the function nodes involved in the cycle as many times as the maximal loop count.

**DYNAMIC WEB SERVICE INVOCATION - ADVANCED**

**1. Headers**

Besides parameters, a web service operation may include "headers". Headers are basically additional parameters that are carried inside the header of a SOAP request/response instead of in the body. In general headers are used to specify additional information not strictly related to the semantics of an operation such a as the credentials (username and password) required to invoke it.

The WSData class allows managing parameters and headers homogeneously: while the

void setParameter(<parameter-name>, < parameter-value>)
AbsObject getParameter(<parameter-name>)
String getParameterString(<parameter-name>),
int getParameterInteger(<parameter-name>),
boolean getParameterBoolean(<parameter-name>)
...

methods are available to manage parameters, the

void setHeader(<header-name>, <header-value>)
AbsObject getHeader(<header-name>)
String getHeaderString(<header-name>)
integer getHeaderInteger(<header-name>)
boolean getHeaderBoolean(<header-name>)
...

methods are available to manage headers.

## 2. Proxy

In many cases both the access to a WSDL (at DynamicClient initialization time) and the actual web service invocation require passing through an HTTP Proxy. The DynamicClient class provides the following methods to set proxy information.

☐ setProxyHost(<host>): Set the proxy host (e.g. 163.162.10.12)

☐ setProxyPort(<port>): Set the proxy port (e.g. 8080)

☐ setNonProxyHosts(<listOfAddresses>): Set a list of addresses (possibly including '*') that will be accessed without using the proxy. The separator is the '|' character

☐ setProxyAuthentication(<user>, <password>): Set the credentials (if any) required to access the proxy

The following code snipped provides an example.

dc.**setProxyHost**("10.12.175.14");
dc.**setProxyPort**("8080");
dc.**setNonProxyHosts**("163.163.*|*.telecomitalia.it");
dc.**setProxyAuthentication**("myUser", "myPwd");
dc.initClient(new URI("http://myWSDL"));

## 3. Security

Certain web services require HTTP Basic Authentication. The DynamicClient class provides the following methods to set HTTP related information.

☐ setDefaultHttpUsername(): Specifies the http username used in all requests.

☐ setDefaultHttpPassword(): Specifies the http password used in all requests.

The following code snipped provides an example.
dc.**setDefaultHttpUsername**("MyHttpUsername");
dc.**setDefaultHttpPassword**("MyHttpPassword");
If the credential of HTTP Basic Authentication are different in all requests is possible specify them in invoke(…) method with SecurityProperties object.
Instead, if the credential of HTTP Basic Authentication are different for the WSDL discovery is possible specify them in initClient(…) method.
The following code snipped provides an example
dc.**initClient**(new URI("http://myWSDL"), "MyHttpUsername", "MyHttpUsername");
Other web services require WS-Security Username Token. The DynamicClient class provides the following methods to set WSS related information.
 setDefaultWSSUsername(): Specifies the wss username used in all requests.
 setDefaultWSSPassword(): Specifies the wss password used in all requests.
 setDefaultWSSPasswordType(): Specifies the wss password type used in all requests (TEXT or DIGEST, see SecurityProperties object).

The following code snipped provides an example.
dc.**setDefaultWSSUsername**("MyWSSUsername");
dc.**setDefaultWSSPassword**("MyWSSPassword");
dc.**setDefaultWSSPasswordType**(SecurityProperties.PW_TEXT);
If the credential of WS-Security Username Token are different in all requests is possible specify them in invoke(…) method with SecurityProperties object.
Other web services require WS-Security Timestamp. The DynamicClient class provides the following method to set WSS related information.
 setDefaultWSSTimeToLive(): Specifies the wss request time to live (in second) used in all requests.

The following code snipped provides an example.
dc.**setDefaultWSSTimeToLive**(60);
If the credential of WS-Security Timestamp are different in all requests is possible specify them in invoke(…) method with SecurityProperties object.
Other web services require SSL connections with or without certificates. The DynamicClient class provides the following methods to set SSL related information.
 enableCertificateChecking(): Enables the certificates checking mechanism. When this mechanism is enabled (the default situation) a trust store holding certificates of trusted remote servers must be indicated (see the setTrustStore() method).
 disableCertificateChecking(): Disables the certificate checking mechanism.

☐ setTrustStore(<file.keystore>): Specifies the keystore holding certificates of trusted remote servers

☐ setTrustStorePassword(<password>): Specifies the password used to protect the keystore of trusted certificates

The following code snipped provides an example.

```
dc.setTrustStore("C:/myFolder/cert.keystore");
dc.setTrustStorePassword("myPassword");
dc.initClient(new URI("http://myWSDL"));
```

## 4. Caching

Considering that the initialization of a DynamicClient (initClient() method) is a long operation that may take some seconds, a good approach is to create a single DynamicClient instance for each WSDL and reuse it whenever an operation of a service described in that WSDL must be invoked (note that the invoke() methods of the DynamicClient class are thread safe and therefore can be called by two or more threads in parallel). In order to facilitate this practice the WSDC provides a class called DynamicClientCache that manages all issues related to creation, initialization and caching of DynamicClient objects in a thread safe mode. The DynamicClientCache class follows the singleton pattern and therefore the first step when using it is to retrieve the singleton DynamicClientCache instance by means of the getInstance() method.

The following code snippet shows how to use the DynamicClientCache class.

```
DynamicClientCache dcc = DynamicClientCache.getInstance();
DynamicClient client = dcc.get(new URI("http://myWSDL"));
......
WSData output = client.invoke("sum", input);
```

The get() method of the DynamicClientCache class first checks if a DynamicClient object was already created to access the given WSDL and returns it in that case. Only if no DynamicClient object is already available a new one is created and initialized.

## CONCLUSION:

Our objective has been to address service selection in the context of a QoS-aware middleware for dynamic service environments. To do so we have proposed an approach which at first by using the CBA algorithm, aims to classify the candidate web services to different QoS levels, differentiate the services within each class, respect to their distances from the user's demand for the QoS criterion. By this classification a utility value is defined for each service that shows its relative importance We have studied the problem of service selection with multiple QoS constraints and proposed several algorithms. The selection of dynamic web service is depends upon the Execution price, Execution duration, Reputation, Successful execution rate, Availability, response time $\leq$ 600,cost $\leq$ 250,availability $\geq$ 85%.

## REFERENCES:

[1]. Towards Efficient Selection of Web Services
Amir Padovitz
School of Computer Science &
Software Engineering,
Monash University
Padovitz@bigpond.com
Shonali Krishnaswamy
School of Computer Science &
Software Engineering,
Monash University
shonali.krishnaswamy@
mail.csse.monash.edu.au
Seng Wai Loke
School of Computer Science &
Software Engineering,
Monash University
swloke@csse.monash.edu.au
[2]. Dynamic Selection of Web Services with Recommendation System
Umardand Shripad Manikrao
Indian Institute of Technology, Kanpur
shripad@cse.iitk.ac.in
T.V.Prabhakar
Indian Institute of Technology, Kanpur
tvp@cse.iitk.ac.in
[3] World Wide Web Consortium (2000/2001): Web Services,
eXtended Markup Language (XML),
Simple Object Access Protocol (SOAP), Web Services
Description Language (WSDL)
Available at: 4.1 http://www.w3.org/TR/ws-gloss/, 4.2
http://www.w3.org, 4.3 http://www.w3.org/TR
[4] Evren Sirin, Bijan Parsia, and James Hendler. "Filtering
and Selecting Semantic Web Services with Interactive
Composition Techniques", IEEE Intelligent
Systems, 19(4):42-49, 2004.
[5] DAML Technical Committee. DARPA Agent Markup
Language- DAML. http://www.daml.org
[6] Prashant Doshi, Richard Goodwin, Rama
Akkiraju. "Parameterized Semantic Matching
for Workflow Composition", IBM Research
Report,RC23133(W0403-026),March, 2004.
[7] M. Paolucci et al. "Semantic Matching of Web Services
Capabilities", The Semantic Web-ISWC 2003:
1st Int'l Semantic Web Conf., LNCS 2342, Springer-
Verlag, 2002, p.333.
[8] Badrul Sarwar, George Karypis, Joseph Konstan, and
John Riedl. "Item-based Collaborative Filtering Recommendation
Algorithms". In the Proceedings of the
10 International World Wide Web Conference. Hong
Kong, 2001.
[9] Daniel Lemire, Sean McGrath. "Implementing a
Rating-Based Item-to-Item Recommender System in
PHP/SQL", Technical Report D-01, January, 2005.
[10] Efficient Algorithms for Web Services
Selection with End-to-End QoS Constraints
TAO YU, YUE ZHANG, and KWEI-JAY LIN University of California, Irvine.